Funny Thoughts

Funny thoughts spin through my mind,

Strangest things of every kind.

They tumble, twist, and never stop,

Sometimes I laugh; sometimes I drop.

They circle round, then loop and play,

Crashing through my busy day.

But then I think of Nolan bright,

That happy child, my heart's delight.

I run to see his smiling face,

To laugh, to play, to feel his grace.

And in that moment, wild thoughts cease.

With him, my world is full of peace.

Follow Me

Follow me.

I'm not quite sure where I'm going,

But if you follow me up a tree,

We'll surely see

The world in front of you and me.

Maybe it won't be clear

Which way we ought to go,

But follow me,

Just follow me,

And we will see.

Grandma Libby

I am not the ordinary type,

As you will soon find out.

I won't fit inside a box.

Of that, there is no doubt.

I won't step in front of you

Or jump over your words.

You can sing out loud, off-key if you please.

Let your spirit be heard.

Jump in puddles, muddy feet.

Color outside the lines.

I just ask you to be you.

And let me be extraordinary too.

Words Falling Out

Tumbling, spilling out of my mouth.

How do I stop it?

I have no idea.

Why did I start?

I do not know.

Mommy says she couldn't wait for my first words.

Now she says,

Please stop talking.

Please stop talking.

I hear it again.

Hush hush hush.

Hush now.

Don't talk in church.

Don't talk in the elevator.

Don't talk to strangers.

She was so happy when I said *Mama*.

So proud when I said *Dada*.

My first words!

Now she just tells me to

Hush hush.

Hush my mouth.

Still, words keep falling

Right out of my mouth.

I laugh and giggle.

She smiles back at me.

Coloring Out of the Lines

The teacher says to color by number.

Each number has a color.

But I don't want to.

I want to do it my way.

I hope the teacher understands

That I color outside the lines.

I move the crayon or pencil

The way it feels.

It definitely frees my mind.

So if you feel like coloring,

It's okay to color

Especially out of lines.

Who Said?

Who said you can't do it?
Who said it can't be done?
Who dares to doubt your fire—
Your rising with the sun?

You better run, run far away
From the ones who say you can't.
Get closer to the voices
That cheer you on, that chant:

"Come on and run, run!
Let your spirit rise and sing."
Who said you can't do it?
They don't know a thing.

Go on your way.
Be bold, be strong.
I did.
I've been running all along.

Fancy Words

Do fancy words make you smart?

Or does it really matter?

Do fancy words make you rich?

Or does it really matter?

I don't have fancy words to say.

I'm just an ordinary one

Throughout the day.

And maybe that's okay.

Little one,

Come on now.

Let's go off!

And play!

Morning Birds

Waking early to the birds,

They whistle clear,

In different tunes.

I listen, though I know

They're far—

Up in the tree, not where we are.

Each one sings a song, its own,

A melody in joy alone.

Lovely songs that lift the day,

In their own sweet,

Feathery way.

Tippy Tippy Toes

I watch you on your tippy toes,

Moving fast, the way it goes.

Never walking, never slow.

Always running, off you go.

Just like Grandpa Tommy too.

On his tippy toes he flew—

Checking wheels, so quick, so free,

A lively trait passed down to thee.

How lucky you are, little one,

To carry what your grandpa's done.

Tippy tippy toes that show,

His spirit lives in where you go.

All Seven of Them

All seven of them, seven poodles true,

Hearts full of love in red, blue hues too.

They line up in order, eager and bright,

Ready to please and bring pure delight.

I open the door with a laugh and a cheer.

They bound out the door, wild and free without fear.

Dashing and jumping 'round the palm trees so grand,

Their playful parade a sight so unplanned.

They twirl in their circles, a dance full of grace,

Until one elegant poodle pauses in place.

A leg raised just so, marking his little decree.

I chuckle and murmur, "Thank you kindly."

Not in the house, for that space I must spare.

Outdoors is their kingdom, with fresh open air.

A spot for a pee or a cheeky poop too,

For my dear kitchen would suffer if left askew.

My seven poodles, a joyful, free team,

Running and romping like a vivid daydream.

At last I have found where I truly belong—

In this lively chaos, where all hearts grow strong.

I Go Out

I wake up early to start my day.

I go out in a cheerful way.

But it doesn't always work that way.

I stop and smile, then say hello

And gently let my puppies go.

Charlie, Mavis, Susie too,

They know just what to do.

They lick the tears and wag their tails.

And soon that frown begins to fail.

A little joy, a little play—

I know they helped to lift their day.

Swimming!

They put me in the water

To see what I would do.

I flapped my hands.

I swallowed too.

I truly know—

I hated you.

But I needed to know

What I could do.

So I tried and tried,

and then tried some more.

Now I'm the top lifeguard

Standing on the shore.

Ha!

Today I look out,

Strong and free—

Wow.

My mommy was right...

Look at me.

Where We Come From

Great Grandpa Joe chills from Italy.

Grandma Sylvia—can you see?

She is far away from there.

She comes from Poland, full of care.

Great Grandpa Leo—Poland, too.

With Grandma close, they both came through.

Russia, Romania, Iceland's snow—

So many places people go.

America, America—

That's all I know,

America is where the families grow.

People come from far and wide.

From talking different talks, they try.

America, America—the home to be,

For every heart that wants to be free.

The Wind, The Wind

The wind, the wind, the wind goes.

It pulls its way, and then it goes.

The things you see: the leaves, the trees,

The branches sway in drifting breeze.

And maybe me—yes, maybe me.

So wild, so free,

It pulls me gently, ever near

Toward my home, where all is clear.

Why Is There Bedtime?

Wake up and catch the sun,

But bedtime isn't fun.

I run around the house,

Hoping she won't catch me!

I don't mind a pillow,

Soft beneath my head,

But I'd rather jump and twirl

Than lie still in my bed.

Oh, why is there bedtime?

Why must I count sheep?

I guess I'm getting tired.

I guess I need some sleep.

Write Your Own

It doesn't matter what you own.

Pick up a pen; pick up a phone.

Write your stories, long or short.

It doesn't matter, it's just your thought.

Say it loud. Say it strong.

Even with a quiet song.

But don't forget:

It's yours all along.

A is for Alyssa, who shines always bright.
D is for David, strong, walking with delight.

Sharon and David, his parents so dear,
Both from New York City, they bring love near.

They love Devil Dogs and Suzy Q's too.
But their grandson Nolan is sweeter than two!

Now all together, side by side,
The Bosio family—a name filled with pride.

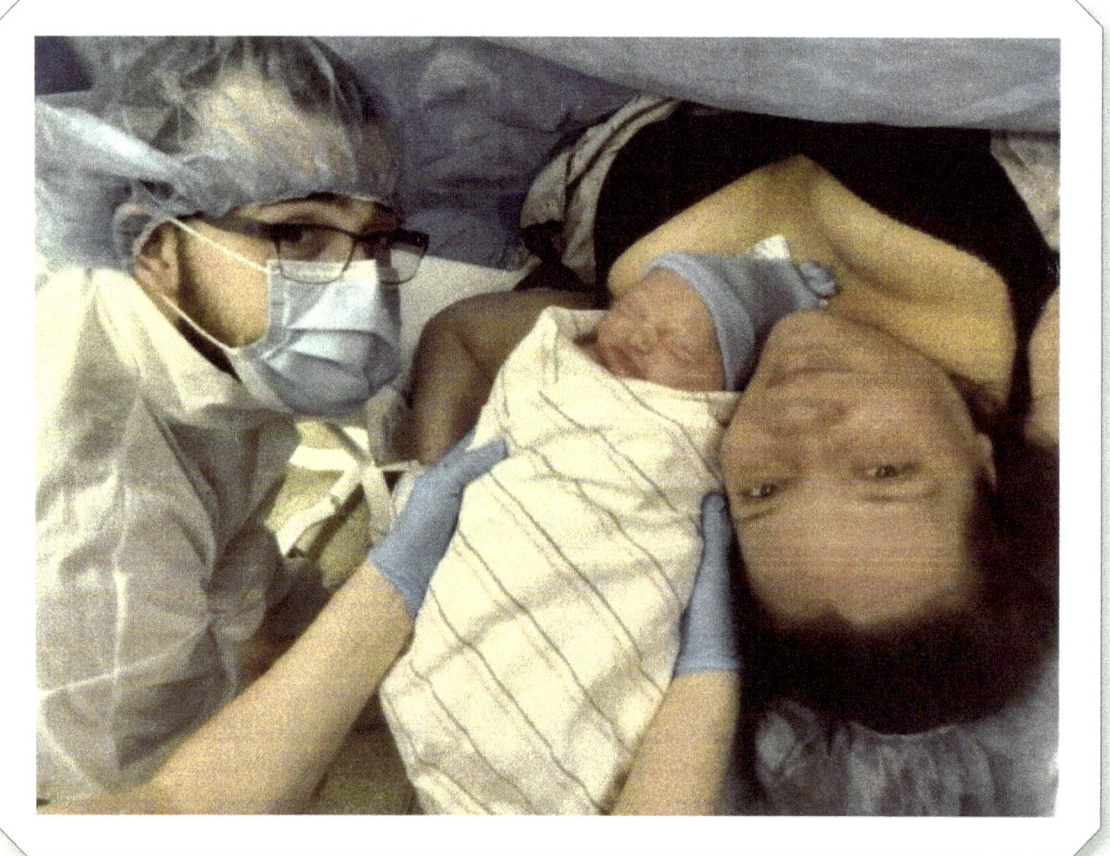

© 2026 by Tara Ellen Debra

All rights reserved. No part of this publication may be reproduced or transmitted in any form or by any means, electronic or mechanical, including photocopying, recording, or any other information storage and retrieval system, without the written permission of the author or publisher.

Printed in the United States of America. Published in Hellertown, PA

ISBN 979-8-89420-078-1

Library of Congress Control Number available upon request.

www.ingramcontent.com/pod-product-compliance
Lightning Source LLC
Chambersburg PA
CBHW060655060526
44119CB00076B/264